THE WALL & BEY

*To John Dick,
with gratitude
for his poetic input ;)*

Irene Kunowski

02/25/2013

THE WALL & BEYOND

poems by

JOANNA KUROWSKA

Copyright 2013 by Joanna Kurowska
All rights reserved

Cover Design: Joanna Kurowska

ISBN-13: 978-1482371178
ISBN-10: 1482371170

Published by
eLectio Publishing, LLC
Little Elm, TX

ACKNOWLEDGMENTS

Versions of some of the poems inluded in this collection originally appeared in the following publications:

Apple Valley Review: "The Ant"; "In A Train"; "Joseph Conrad"; "Singing in Polish";

Bateau: "It"; "Near"

Concise Delight: "To The Priest"

Dappled Things: "Tabernacle"

Illuminations: *** (in Ożarowo, in my grandma's room...)

International Poetry Review: "The Disappearance of Mark S."; "A Dream"; "Mistake"; "The Wall's Corner"

*ken*again:* "Incarnation"; "Stained Glass"

Penwood Review: "Faith"; "The Moment"

Pisarze.pl (Poland): "The Disappearance of Mark S."; "Joseph Conrad"; "Ten Years Ago in Olsztyn"; "The Wall's Corner"

Room Magazine: "A Confession"; "The Wall Games"

Strong Verse: "Missionary of Love"; "A Sparrow"

A NOTE OF APPRECIATION

The following is a collection of poems written originally in Polish. After my immigration to the United States in 1988, I gradually switched to English as my poetic medium. I also translated most of my Polish poems. Friends and teachers helped me in this process, through their encouragement and advice. I am especially grateful to Dr. Donald G. Marshall, my former academic advisor, wonderful teacher of English, and patient reader. I would like to thank my fiancé John Brownell, whose unfailing encouragement as well as his suggestions regarding the choice of the best English idiom have been indispensable in preparing this collection. Special thanks to my son Paul Mlynarczyk for letting me use two of his photographs (the wall and the bird) for my cover design. Finally, I would like to thank my friends who believed in me as a poet: my parents Halina and Bohdan Kurowski, my son Paul, Anita Cukier, Dr. Marina Cap-Bun, Dr. Jennifer Day, John Dick, Dr. Andrzej Gałowicz, Dr. Jerzy Kolodziej, Dr. Ariann Stern-Gottschalk, and Maria Zakrzewska.

TABLE OF CONTENTS

It	1
*** (In Ożarowo…)	2
Stained Glass	3
in a train	4
a carol	5
A Dream	6
"Under Atlas" Café	7
Cloto	8
Separation	9
A Sparrow	10
The Passage	11
To The Priest	12
Faith	13
A Warning	14
God	15
Catechesis	16
Tabernacle	17
*** (beetles' colorful wings…)	18
To R.B.	19
The Hell	20
The Wall	21
A Confession	22
Poland 1991	23
The Disappearance of Mark S.	24
In A Train	25
Babel	26
The Ant	27
Singing in Polish	28
Joseph Conrad	29
An Angel	30
In Poland, 1993	31
Ten Years Ago in Olsztyn	32
Near	33
The Wall Games	34
church	35
Dressed Up	36
Theology	37

*** (Reading an obituary…)	38
Mistake	39
Incarnation	40
*** (one day, the roughcast…)	41
The Wall's Corner	42
Ode To The River	43
A Moment	44
veneer	45
*** (perhaps He collects us…)	46
The Wall's Prayer	47
*** (after many years I discovered…)	48
Don't be afraid	49
Mother	50
Missionary of Love	51
Salvation	52
*** (today when the wind blows…)	53

It

first it is cornflower-blue
it is round, open wide,
straightened up, understanding nothing

then it ceases moving
it thickens into a plaster cast
surrounded by a rough wall

suddenly it turns pink
it digs with its soft hand
into the nooks of childhood

then it bounces its aching head
against the white ribs of death,
still amazed at itself

* * *

In Ożarowo, in my Grandma's room
the lilies smelled intoxicating.

On the wall hung a picture
of the Virgin Mary in a blue gown.

Grandma knelt down and prayed
in time with the bugs' evening music.

I pulled down my pajamas
and, laughing, jumped on the bed.

You godless creature! cried Grandma
her voice trembling with holy wrath.

Her fury matched the offense.
The devil rubbed his hairy hands.

Stained Glass

mark cries loud

in the train, an old woman nibbles on a bun

eva washes her long copper hair
in the karaśnik lake

the wolves howl
inside the stove's throat

in a train

people caught in oddity,
bashful, open their faces
and cast around
little question-hooks

they catch nothing
save identical faces
of other passengers wrapped up
in wall-like silence

a carol

the snow is squeaking tiny bells are ringing
a priest is paying his christmas visits
the tenant-building is holiday-clean

cakes, soap, and pine trees smell
over the doors, crucifixes swell
praised-be-for-ever-and-ever, everywhere

only the old woman on the third floor
keeps her door locked with three bolts

too weak to tidy up, now she is sitting
and weeping that she has missed
her ticket to nonexistence

A Dream

In my dream the bus stops at the cemetery
the moon is at the very heart of concentric circles

a crumb of the apocalypse
suddenly tears from it

sunset light is dripping from above
black smoke is crawling through the streets of the town

my college friends from Toruń, and my aunt
are waiting for the end of the world

get in they say there is still one more seat

"Under Atlas" Café

Our baby brother No
was growing up next to us
but we noticed him only
when he became everything

Our homes built inward
bore negative numbers
Time reverted to its
mythical beginnings

We rejected the world
starting with the word Yes;
when, in "Under Atlas" café,
we talked of unknown freedom

Whispering impenetrably,
our poets read fate
inscribed on the bottoms
of their wine glasses

Our dreams were
connected to nothing,
so the wind blowing backward
carried them away

In the end, only No stayed with us.
Now we turn our mirror-faces
and together look at the world
blooming somewhere

Cloto

In a bar on Mokotowska street
in the half-gloom of a naked bulb,
a blurry-eyed woman
swathed in the blue cocoon
of the nineteen-seventies

stares at me tirelessly

Through the holes in her black coat
her finger-knots crawl out
She moves them one by one
weaving an invisible thread

You will suffer, she says

This very moment time,
suddenly deprived
of its eschatological end,
bends into a circle

Separation

for T.

it is dark, not a sound can be heard
the door has closed so quietly
we will not go together to the place
where the earth is nailed to heaven
the light that penetrates to nonexistence
will not embrace us.

A Sparrow

They talked about pain
until the time of silence came
The wind moved the curtain
A sparrow sat on a twig
and chirped

Somebody asked:
"What are you doing here,
little one?"
He sang:
"For this I entered the world,
that I might testify to truth"

The Passage

The phrase scatters its sounds like leaves,
the tree touches heaven with its crown.
The fugue is Jacob's ladder for me.
On it, angels come down to my heart.

Under the roof, the wind roars its tune
but the fiddler hears only himself.
Someone has passed by me, I'm not sure,
is it a star twinkling out in space?

I'm in the dark—my mind is buried,
eyes filled with dirt, heart sewn to the sand.
The phrase scatters its sounds in the air
but not angels; and the wind has died.

To The Priest

Speak a word to me, father
I need your teaching
for what slips through your fingers,
chases me at night
For I, too, have tasted of the bread
you have chosen
Look, a rainbow above us
—the rain's prayer

Faith

I believe in the silence of the invisible God
creator of the universe
and in the quiet after prayer

I believe in the Teacher's absence in
a half-broken reed and
a dying candle

A Warning

Johann Tauler, the mystic of Rhine,
the nightingale from the Emperor tale,
alighted on my tree-branch.
I heard him singing.
The mountains melted, the waters swelled,
the souls of the dead whirled in the harmony of the spheres.

Unfortunately, he flew down from heaven,
with which I was supposed to remain
in a relationship of contention.
"Are you reading Tauler? That's dangerous,"
said the guardian angel
in a black cassock.

God

in the overall grayness
the smudge of his face
puts on a warm brown

his two words
pronounced sound by sound
are not from this world

Catechesis

No one has ever seen God
but there are rumors
he plays soccer
on the Elysian fields.

According to unbelievable sources
he plays "saved and damned"
twenty four hours a day,
watching every move made by the players
whom he creates on the spot.

Without missing, God hits
into one goal and then the other.
The strings of the nets respond with a moan:
"saved," "condemned."

Tabernacle

there is no such calm
that would not disturb the silence

thoughts die out like candles
that the wind has blown

one cannot come in here
on the tips of one's thoughts

one can only go out from here
to take a break, for example

or eat an apple

* * *

beetles' colorful wings
leaves' webs
fingerprints
autumn colors' profusion
water's intricacy
clouds' endless shapes
rocks' abundance
aquarium fish's variety
many colors of skin
potpourri of human faces
but only one religion?

To R. B.

Catholicism became a harbor for you
a final port in which you landed
a freight-arc full of Hebraic names
under the finger-greased sails of the Bible

what gentle breeze had blown in your favor
that you came ashore in a Christian port
along with the six million stigmas
and one single cross?

The Hell

the light has grown stronger
liver spots, germs, and all the angles
of the chair and the table
have come to light

the interiors
of the bed and armchair
have poured out
the contrast on tv
has improved

all is visible
except the door
only rats under the floor
know the way out

in the corner a man
who is nothing but despair
in heaven a god
who is nothing but love

The Wall

The wall is straight black seemingly humble
built on a rock motionless
it stands with dignity on man's way

when you touch it cold penetrates you
when you look at it from up-close
its beauty begins to overwhelm you

The wall climbs up under the sky stretching high;
blind and deaf it does not know at all
if it will be able to justify its existence

So before you grow numb, yourself becoming a wall
you begin to understand that it too
is full of despair

A Confession

When I bring my mouth close to the wall's ear
I feel cold and perceive a stone heartbeat.
Shells of pain, turned into bullets of sins,
bounce against the rough plaster and return to me.

In the mirror, I see an ear-shaped face
with no mouth to shout, no eyes to cry.
It is I—a helpless conch, a mute shell; open
to anything that crawls in from outside.

Poland 1991

they tore off our coats
and our crown of thorns
Down fell the garments of slavery
in which we looked dignified
attracting everyone's attention

from underneath
a sweaty gray shirt emerged,
matches and a cork-screw in the pocket
in the purse, torn at the corner,
an American quarter
carefully saved for many years

The Disappearance of Mark S.

Our schoolmate
Mark S.
disappeared
the Beast had kidnapped him
to make him her servant

So abruptly did he vanish from our lives
our street our town
our ours we us
he was no more

After some time there arrived
the terrifying news
that he worked very hard
and could no longer drink beer

Later on, there came a mysterious cipher
full of exotic words
such as *fak* and *wery łel*
and a package containing
pinatbater and chewing gum

By and by, Mark changed
into a plaster statue
before which men take off their hats
and women decorate with flowers,
later to bring before it
their wailing supplications

We stay firm in our belief
that Mark will return to us
grace-famous

In A Train

I could not find a way
to convince the conductor
that I had the ticket
using my finger I tried
to point to my heart and my mouth

he towered over me
a scarecrow
one I was scared of
in my childhood

he finally said: *you may go*

the train is rolling and rolling
I hear the wheels rattle
you may you may not

Babel

I've built a skyscraper
a thousand skyscrapers
to escape the blue butterfly
the shape of his wings is too simple
and I'm afraid of secret words
far below the little butterfly has stayed
he flies over a brook over a flower
christ is waving his little blue wings
he won't fly up here—he won't

The Ant

it appears in a train
between Fullerton and Belmont

makes hunger constrict
the arteries of my body-nest

it crawls stubbornly, full of faith
that I am a dark forest

a fiery-red longing, it eats
into my thoughts' corridors

Singing in Polish

The morning *shower*
(this word is important
like the fragrance of the soap
that dresses me
in a foreign skin
the same fragrance
that used to be only
a postcard from abroad)
Incautiously
I hummed a song
that was like a figure
cut from a holy picture
without the halo
The morning *shower*
washes away the remnants of illusions
I am but an abysmal stomach
crying to be fed.

Joseph Conrad

For Don Marshall

In a broken jar, the sea leaks through the cracks.
Sailors despair; nothing rocks them anymore.
The gristmill of time changes aquatic plants,
fish, prayers, and people, into yellow sand.

In a mirror, love watches its image—fright.
Their glances—a bridge stretching into the dark.
A rainbow of faces flicker in the glass;
one of them is yours but you don't know which one.

The spirit hiding in life's seashell is pain.
He is the god-figure that opens the door
and takes you to the earth's heart and the hand's palm
where long forgotten sources flow over stones.

An Angel

To the Fiddler from the tunnel

between State and Dearborn streets
deep underground
there is a tunnel
that one passes through quickly

sometimes
an angel descends to it
makes tall pine trees rustle
lights glitter on water

In Poland, 1993

Again I climb these stairs,
grasping the splinters of the balustrade.

At the turn of the stairs, through an open window, falls
Providence's blue-eyed gaze
bruised on the roofs of townhouses.

I don't know if the stairs are wooden or stone
Time muffles all sound.

When I get to the top, a strange face
jumps out from behind the door, like a mean dog,
to bite me with a polite
They don't live here any more.

Ten Years Ago in Olsztyn

ten years ago
my grandpa was dying
the guards of the hospital did not allow him
to see his great-grandson

my father—political prisoner
locked up with a rapist and a murderer—
reflected on the price
of his conversion

the prosecutor Ihadto
was following orders
so he withheld correspondence
and refused visitations

the secret police read
my intimate letters;
Paweł cried during the search,
Mom they are messing up my toys!

Aunt Ewa prayed so much
that God touched her heart
Seized by mystical fear,
it stopped beating

mother entered a new world
in which colors spoke
and reality changed
into a foreign tongue

the people walked to the cemetery
the remains of Marcin Antonowicz
Then long into the night they sang
"My Fatherland"

      1995

Near

in a train, a man is sitting near me
his face sunburned but gray
a scar on his forehead
I see clearly—he is near
near a house's door left ajar
near a streak of light on the snow
near a meadow and a forest
near laughter and crying
The whole train in which we are sitting together
is near—and it will ride past
it will go by

The Wall Games

I opened my eyes—the wall was gone
only hot air shimmering
Then, there was a window; outside
a green garden, tree, gooseberry bush

Behind me, a lion-legged table set
The furniture grew self-assured
Mother, dressed in a silk costume
was serving food, hiding her tears

Uncle reached for the bread; I saw
the golden stripes of his uniform
I turned back, the future was there
Someone let me into the room

Someone conferred hurriedly with another
under a lampshade. It was a dark night
I came closer, my hand crumpling the invitation
I bumped my face against transparent glass

church

in a stone wall
a blue stained-glass

the cross of the winds,
transparent

Dressed Up

the wall does not come forward
it smiles in the door, refined

its polished eye glittering,
it puts on a white shirt
and a silk tie

it decorates itself with a cross,
all the saints, a mother of god

it knows well gospel's tender love
becomes it

Theology

Words—green algae
the rash of leaves and water lilies
sermons' fleshy flowers
greatness' breeze

Harmony—seemingly
but immersing yourself you feel
that leaves are fastened to long, twisted stems
amid sticky waterweeds

Everything rises and falls
as befitting the nature of things:
fat fish, argument-leeches, the weight of feet
sinking deeper and deeper in slime

* * *

Reading an obituary
in a Catholic weekly
I become aware that
I won't be promoted
to a reverend infulate,
a territorial prelate,
a vicar general, or
a prefect apostolic.
No one will require
of me an oath before
my incardination;
unlikely a canon prelate
will anoint me for
my last journey;
a dean of a decanate
will not bid me farewell.
It remains unknown if I
will be admitted to
the kingdom of heaven

Mistake

Mistake, how would I dare
speak directly to you
when you appear dressed in crimson
and step with the dignity
of many centuries.
Your hands are white, smelling of soap;
in speaking you use secret words
drawn from the *Summa Theologiae*
and the Roman Missal.
In the evening you fold
your stole, alb, and cassock on a chair.
You hang your biretta on a hanger,
along with your gray, coiffed hair.
On your nightstand you put away
your hands smelling of soap.
Suddenly you have taken the shape
of a little wet bird
shivering with fear.

Incarnation

the wall sometimes becomes human
it covers itself with a coat of skin,
puts on gloves of hands

when you touch it, it accepts the caress
motionless—smooth and hot
lofty like the August sky

you must push your hand deeper still
into the crevice where the heart throbs
to feel the fangs of cold

the wall is creeping forward and up and sideways
in silence interrupted only
by the rustling of stony scruples

* * *

one day, the roughcast
of plaster and flesh will fall off

the wall will stand naked
and transparent

there will be only you

and chunks of people
laboriously crawling
onto the other side of me
a hair strand, for example, or a finger

that, which I will have saved

The Wall's Corner

when the wall meets itself
it stares at itself in amazement
first with its right eye then its left

immediately, it feels hostility
but not right away does it change into stone
the object of its stare

it knows not what name to give
that which is seizing it over
from its very foundations

Ode To The River

river if you stopped just for a moment
then the fish, shot into space
like a wise eye stuck in a blue aureole,
would nail me to the spot with its gaze

but you take all the fish away
you install a void in every eye
you disguise all in a face different
from the one I had no time to recognize

A Moment

I am here just for a moment
I won't manage to see
the Cathedral in Rheims
and all those places
with such sonorous names
that poets like.
But will I manage to take a step
toward the door
and my neighbor?
Will I name
for the first time
the color of the window frame
and the asphalt breaking down the light?
That which is nearest, because
to the tree and the stone
I won't make it
in time.

I have made my mark in the snow
I have seen a nail, bent in the fence
in front of a church that was growing slowly
up from the bristle
of scaffolds
And I opened my mouth
it is not clear why
to catch a breath
or to say the word:

finis

veneer

we cover death with eternity
dressed in a black shining stone
that is smooth
and does not stick to the hands

we cover eternity with life
dressed in the bright colors of flowers
smelling sweet

we cover life with ever-burning fire
of tomb-candles

* * *

perhaps He collects us like butterflies
pinned to the wall of eternity,
studying how we flail our limbs
in the display-case of freedom

The Wall's Prayer

the wall is kneeling and saying "Our Father"
it is hard to know if feet can hear it
or if its plaster thought reaches knee level

much less the cosmos
if there is a cosmos
beyond the wall

the wall is kneeling and saying "Our Father"
as if it were surrounded by something more
than plaster infinity

* * *

after many years I discovered
in the earth's monastic cell
that light is everywhere
under many names

it is enough to walk on the edge
of the barred window-shelf
face up to the wind
that blows from the sea

Don't be afraid

Don't be afraid of the love
that pains only you
but run away from the one
that hurts others

The one that pains you is good
make it your strength
accept it—then you will become
as clear as a crystal

You will be an open window
a light in the dark

Mother

Mother lies down in the grave together with her child.
She cannot tear herself from this bundle of matter.
Then she rises to live on—a sign of resurrection.
She is the first to conquer death; her love
lives on both sides of the umbilical cord.

When the child that is a question mark dies
mother already knows the answer.
Blindfolded, she goes into eternity.
If there is no eternity, she creates it

Missionary of Love

Don't worry
I have not come
to yell the names of things unknown
into your ear

I will not be
attaching a beard to God's face
or putting glasses on yours

I have come to ask
for a little bit of room

Salvation

With the wand of my sight I touch
the beam
captured by Indian summer

Secretly, from under my bench, I eat
yogurt
bought on the way to school

With a caressing touch, I smooth
the crochets
hidden in the credenza

thanking them
for salvation

* * *

Today when the wind blows
I bow my head and say nothing

The wind remains silent, too
It makes no promises

It is the wind

ABOUT THE AUTHOR

JOANNA KUROWSKA published poetry in *American Tanka*, *Apple Valley Review*, *Bateau*, *Christianity & Literature*, *Concise Delight*, *Dappled Things*, *The Green Door*, *Illuminations*, *International Poetry Review*, *ken*again*, *Oklahoma Review*, *Penwood Review*, *Room Magazine*, *Solo Novo*, *Strong Verse*, *Vineyards,* and *Write From Wrong Magazine.* Her poetry collection *Inclusions* is forthcoming from Červená Barva Press. Previously, Joanna published two books of poetry in Poland, *Ściana* : The Wall, 1997; and *Obok* : Near, 1999. Her Polish poems appeared also in journal publications, including *Kultura* (Paris) and *Fraza* (Rzeszów, Poland). Joanna holds a doctorate in literature from the University of Illinois at Chicago (2007) and her critical works appeared in *Anglican Theological Review*, *The Conradian* (forthcoming); *Joseph Conrad Today*, *NewPages*, *Sarmatian Review*, *Slavic and East European Journal*, and elsewhere. She has taught at American universities, including Indiana University, Bloomington, IN, and the University of Chicago.

The Wall & Beyond has been first published as an eBook, by eLectio Publishing, 2012.

Made in the USA
Lexington, KY
12 February 2013